Jacob's Ladder

Reading Comprehension Program

Second Edition

Grade

3

Student Workbook
Poetry

Contributing Editors:
Joyce VanTassel-Baska,
Tamra Stambaugh,
Kimberley L. Chandler

Contributing Authors:
Heather French,
Paula Ginsburgh,
Tamra Stambaugh,
Joyce VanTassel-Baska

William & Mary
School of Education
CENTER FOR GIFTED EDUCATION

William & Mary
School of Education
Center for Gifted Education
P.O. Box 8795
Williamsburg, VA 23187

First published in 2017 by Prufrock Press Inc.

Published 2021 by Routledge
605 Third Avenue, New York, NY 10017
2 Park Square, Milton Park, Abingdon, Oxon OX14 4RN

Routledge is an imprint of the Taylor & Francis Group, an informa business

Edited by Lacy Compton

Cover and layout design by Raquel Trevino

ISBN-13: 978-1-61821-731-8

Routledge
Taylor & Francis Group

NEW YORK AND LONDON

Table of Contents

The Sound of Rain 2

Winter Shavings. 4

Owl. 6

Fog 8

Those Days Ago 10

Summer Song 12

Summer in the South 14

Dandelions. 17

Windy Nights. 19

Aloft 21

The Sound of Rain

by Emily Yao

Rain.
Slowly dripping
down, pitter-patter,
pitter-patter,
a musical rhythm
inside my
head.
When I look
up,
glimmers of
light seep through
mad, ferocious
clouds
of black and grey.
When I look
down,
puddles of water
collect
on the mushy, wet grass,
reflecting my

image like a
mirror
on a wall.
A drop falls,
then another,
another,
again and again.
My reflection ripples in a
pool of rain.
Wind whistles and winds
around me,
slapping me on my
cheek.
Rain.
Slowly dripping
down, pitter-patter,
pitter-patter,
a musical rhythm
inside my
head.

Note. Originally published in *Creative Kids* magazine, Spring 2016. Reprinted with permission of Prufrock Press.

THE SOUND OF RAIN

Main Idea, Theme, or Concept

C3   Main Idea: What is the main idea of this poem?

_____

_____

_____

_____

_____

Inference

C2   The author seems to be outside during a storm. What words tell you this?

_____

_____

_____

_____

_____

Literary Elements

C1   What is the author's tone when she writes about rain?

_____

_____

_____

What words tell you this?

_____

_____

_____

_____

Winter Shavings

by Ellen Zhang

A small and naïve child,
With pure white wondering eyes,
Falling, spiraling
Into a blanket,
Of soft silence, rippling
The small snowflake starts
To float slowly
Gravity stops it, but it
Is a snowflake and
It's already frozen

Note. Originally published in *Creative Kids* magazine, Winter 2014. Reprinted with permission of Prufrock Press.

WINTER SHAVINGS

Main Idea, Theme, or Concept

C3   Main Idea: How does the title give the reader a clue about the main idea of the poem? Explain your answer using words from the poem.

_____

_____

_____

_____

Inference

C2   "Winter Shavings" What does the author mean by this title?

_____

_____

What can be inferred about the snowflakes from this title?

_____

_____

Literary Elements

C1   Make a list of phrases or words that describe snow.

_____

_____

_____

_____

How does the author use those words and phrases to put a picture in your head? What do you "see"? Why?

_____

_____

_____

Illustrate your vision of the poem on another piece of paper, based on the descriptive language used.

Owl

by Iris Kreilkamp

The last of the animals
Slip silently into crevices.
The last door closes,
The last light flickers off,
And an ancient song
Fills the air,
Dripping like velvety paint
Over a dark landscape.
The stars open their eyes,
Awakened by this blanket
Of soft, heavy sound.
The owl sings.

Note. Originally published in *Creative Kids* magazine, Summer 2015. Reprinted with permission of Prufrock Press.

OWL

Main Idea, Theme, or Concept

C3   Theme: Write a poem like "Owl" to describe an animal you like.
(Use the poem as your model.)

_____

_____

_____

_____

_____

_____

_____

Inference

C2   What evidence is important for indicating that the animal being
described is an owl?

_____

_____

_____

_____

_____

_____

_____

Literary Elements

C1   What words does the poet use to describe the owl's song?

_____

_____

_____

_____

_____

_____

Fog

By Carl Sandburg

The fog comes
On little cat feet.

It sits looking
Over harbor and city
On silent haunches
And then moves on.

FOG

Generalizations

B3 Can you create a poem that is like this one? Choose one natural element and one animal from the following table to help you.

Natural Elements	Animal
Sun	Dog
Fire	Horse
Wind	Bird
Rain	Fish

Classifications

B2 The author chooses a cat to describe the fog. What characteristics of cats might have made the author choose it? Make a list of these cat characteristics.

_____

_____

_____

_____

Details

B1 Draw a picture that might go along with the poem. Write a sentence to explain your picture.

_____

_____

Those Days Ago

by Anne Cao

Do you remember the time when I was young?
Do you remember the time at the beach?
The splash and crash of the waves on the sand,
Tall sandcastles stood like valiant knights.
The seaweed was a mermaid's hair
Dancing swiftly through the waves.
The ocean shone like glass
Reflecting the heart of the sun.
And now I can reign
Upon the heat of the sand
Along with the crashing waves.
The beach was my kingdom
And I was its queen.

Note. Originally published in *Creative Kids* magazine, Summer 2015. Reprinted with permission of Prufrock Press.

THOSE DAYS AGO

Generalizations

B3 Generalizations are broad ideas that can apply to many situations. Write at least four generalizations you can make about the beach based on the poem and your list and your categories from Questions B2 and B1. You may use the chart below to help organize your ideas.

Generalization	Evidence From the Poem	Evidence From My List

Classifications

B2 Using your list from Question 2 in Section B1, develop categories for items found at the beach. Put each item into a category. How are your categories similar? How are they different?

_____

_____

_____

_____

_____

Details

B1 "Those Days Ago" is about the beach. On your own paper, draw a picture of at least one item described in the poem. Brainstorm a list of items found at the beach. Write down at least 25 on your paper.

Summer Song

by William Carlos Williams

Wanderer moon
smiling a
faintly ironical smile
at this
brilliant, dew-moistened
summer morning,—
a detached
sleepily indifferent
smile, a
wanderer's smile,—
if I should
buy a shirt
your color and
put on a necktie
sky-blue
where would they carry me?

SUMMER SONG

Main Idea, Theme, or Concept

C3   Main Idea: What is the main idea of this poem?

_____

_____

_____

_____

_____

_____

Inference

C2   How does the poet imply that the summer moon is different or special?

_____

_____

_____

What lines from the poem support your inference?

_____

_____

_____

Literary Elements

C1   _Personification_ is a literary term used when writers give human characteristics to objects. Does the moon demonstrate human qualities in this poem? If so, how? Use text from the poem to support your answer.

_____

_____

_____

_____

_____

Summer in the South

by Paul Laurence Dunbar

The oriole sings in the greening grove
As if he were half-way waiting,
The rosebuds peep from their hoods of green,
Timid and hesitating.
The rain comes down in a torrent sweep
And the nights smell warm and piney,
The garden thrives, but the tender shoots
Are yellow-green and tiny.
Then a flash of sun on a waiting hill,
Streams laugh that erst were quiet,
The sky smiles down with a dazzling blue
And the woods run mad with riot.

SUMMER IN THE SOUTH

Consequences and Implications

A3   What if the seasons never changed? What would be the consequences if it were always summer?

_____

_____

_____

What would be the consequences for people if it were always winter?

_____

_____

_____

What does the poem imply about summer in the South? Support your answer.

_____

_____

_____

_____

_____

_____

Cause and Effect

A2   In "Summer in the South," the poet uses personification to give the different items in nature human-like qualities. The poet writes about things that change because summer arrives, such as "the nights smell warm and piney . . ." How does summer change things in nature? How do you know? Use lines from the poem to support your answer.

_____

_____

_____

In one part of the poem, the author wrote: "Streams laugh that erst were quiet." In your opinion, what effect does the change in the streams have?

_____

_____

_____

_____

_____

Sequencing

A1 The events that occur in nature during the summer are an important part of this poem. How does summer begin? How does it progress?

_____

_____

_____

_____

_____

_____

Using the space below, create and illustrate a timeline for the poem, making sure to sequence the events in the correct order.

Dandelions

by Neha Lenin

I am not one of them.

They will not accept me for who I am,
excluded from parties and conversations,
ignored and overlooked;

They leave me to wonder,
am I kind?
am I caring?
am I a good friend?
because I was told
"it's not what's on the outside but the inside that matters."

Or is it just because of my appearance
and inferior background,
that I am treated the way I am?

I am a dandelion in a field of daisies.
I am not popular, I am not one of them.

Note. Originally published in *Creative Kids* magazine, Spring 2017. Reprinted with permission of Prufrock Press.

DANDELIONS

Generalizations

B3 Which word or phrase best explains the poem: (a) friendship or (b) being an individual? Why? Use words from the poem to explain your answer.

_____

_____

_____

_____

_____

Classifications

B2 This poem has some words and phrases that are positive in meaning, and others that are more negative. Classify words or phrases found in the poem into the two groups: positive and negative.

Positive	Negative

Details

B1 Two students were arguing about what the poem meant. One student said it was about dandelions. Another student said the poem was about someone who didn't fit in too well with other children her age. Which student do you believe is correct? Make a list of words or phrases in the poem that help you know.

_____

_____

_____

_____

Windy Nights

By Robert Louis Stevenson

Whenever the moon and stars are set,
Whenever the wind is high,
All night long in the dark and wet,
A man goes riding by.
Late in the night when the fires are out,
Why does he gallop and gallop about?

Whenever the trees are crying aloud,
And ships are tossed at sea,
By, on the highway, low and loud,
By at the gallop he goes, and then
By he comes back at the gallop again.

WINDY NIGHTS

Consequences and Implications

A3   Who is "he" in the poem?

_____

_____

What clues do you have that might imply who "he" is?

_____

_____

Cause and Effect

A2   Wind causes many things to happen. What happens in the poem as a result of wind?

_____

_____

_____

Can you think of other effects that the wind causes?

_____

_____

_____

Sequencing

A1   Which words does the author use multiple times?

_____

_____

_____

Do you think those are important to the order of the poem? Why or why not?

_____

_____

Aloft

by Miranda Sun

Our seabird is the truest ship
He floats on the skies
With feathery sails
And a light keel bone
His tail as a rudder
Friends with the wind
He perches in port
As swift as a current
He carries the ocean's song.

Note. Originally published in *Creative Kids* magazine, Summer 2015. Reprinted with permission of Prufrock Press.

ALOFT

Main Idea, Theme, or Concept

C3 Main Idea: What is the main idea of this poem?

_____

_____

_____

Inference

C2 What evidence from the poem suggests that the author sees the seabird as a graceful animal?

_____

_____

_____

_____

Literary Elements

C1 The author uses a metaphor to compare the seabird to something else. Identify the metaphor. Describe what she is comparing the bird to in the poem.

_____

_____

_____

What other comparisons does she make to strengthen this comparison?

_____

_____

_____

Identify the two similes in the poem.

_____

_____

_____

9781618217318

First published in 2017 by Prufrock Press Inc.

Published 2021 by Routledge
605 Third Avenue, New York, NY 10017
2 Park Square, Milton Park, Abingdon, Oxon OX14 4RN

Routledge is an imprint of the Taylor & Francis Group, an informa business

Copyright ©2017, Center for Gifted Education, William & Mary

Edited by Lacy Compton

Cover and layout design by Raquel Trevino

ISBN-13: 978-1-61821-731-8

NEW YORK AND LONDON